The Wisdom of Trees

The Wisdom of Trees

How Trees Work Together to
Form a Natural Kingdom

Lita Judge

ROARING BROOK PRESS

New York

For **Dave,**
who shares
a **home**
with **me** in
the **deep**
woods

Published by Roaring Brook Press
Roaring Brook Press is a division of Holtzbrinck Publishing Holdings Limited Partnership
120 Broadway, New York, NY 10271 • mackids.com

Library of Congress Cataloging-in-Publication Data
Names: Judge, Lita, author.
Title: The wisdom of trees : how trees work together to form a natural kingdom / Lita Judge.
Description: New York : Roaring Brook Press, [2021]
Includes bibliographical references. | Audience: Ages 5–8 | Audience: Grades K–1
Summary: "A lyrical and informational nonfiction picture book that tells
the story of trees and the hidden ecosystems they create" —Provided by publisher.
Identifiers: LCCN 2020022632 | ISBN 9781250237071 (hardcover)
Subjects: LCSH: Trees—Juvenile literature.
Classification: LCC QK475.8 .J83 2021 | DDC 582.16—dc23
LC record available at https://lccn.loc.gov/2020022632

Our books may be purchased in bulk for promotional, educational, or business use.
Please contact your local bookseller or the Macmillan Corporate and
Premium Sales Department at (800) 221-7945 ext. 5442 or
by email at MacmillanSpecialMarkets@macmillan.com.

First edition, 2021 • Design by Angela Jun and Mercedes Padró
The illustrations for this book were created with watercolor and pencil.
Printed in China by RR Donnelley Asia Printing Solutions Ltd.,
Dongguan City, Guangdong Province

5 7 9 10 8 6 4

A Secret Kingdom

I am a single beech,
but I am not alone.

Together with my fellow trees,
we form a secret kingdom.

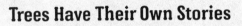

Trees Have Their Own Stories

A young beech grows under a canopy of mature trees in the Ruhe Forest of Hümmel, Germany.

Many tree species, like the beech, live for centuries. Some even survive for thousands of years. The oldest known living tree, a Great Basin bristlecone pine in California, is estimated to be 4,850 years old. Imagine the stories these old trees could tell! But trees don't talk. Or do they?

In recent years, forest ecologists have learned that trees have a secret language all their own, one we can't see or hear, which allows them to work together in communities. The poems in this book reveal what trees might say if they did use words. Trees live longer when they help and defend one another. They can do this only if they communicate. But how does it work?

It begins deep underground.

How to Speak in Tree

Have you learned to speak in tree?
It's very simple, like saying hi.
First find yourself a fungal partner,
but feed him well or he won't help.
Grow together, sharing all,
until your fungi reaches others.
Talk of food, talk of drought,
talk of danger and disease,
becoming bigger than just one tree,
something more, something We.

Secrets of the Wood Wide Web

Near the coast of British Columbia, Canada, a forest of Douglas fir, balsam fir, western hemlock, and western red cedar instant message one another by sending chemical and electrical signals, like secret codes, that travel along mycorrhizal (pronounced "Mike O'Ryzal") fungi living in and around their roots. These fungi branch out in a dense network of straw-like fibers. If we laid the roots of one of these trees out from end to end, they would stretch up to five miles, but their companion fungi would wrap around the earth! Scientists nicknamed this network the Wood Wide Web because of how the fungi allow trees to communicate far beyond their closest neighbors.

Fungi and trees form a symbiotic relationship—each species works with the other to survive. The fungi break down rocks and soil into nutrients, while their tiny tubes help the host tree absorb the nutrients along with more water. In exchange, the tree shares up to a third of the food it makes with the fungi.

Neighbor, Can You Hear Me?

Neighbor, can you hear me?
There are insects on my leaves.
I can taste their saliva
as they nibble,
      nibble,
         nibble.
Neighbor, can you hear me?
Together we must act!
Call the deadly wasp
to help us fight them back.

Counterattacks

Trees may look like passive bystanders, but if attacked, they aren't afraid to fight back. Within Central Park in New York City, an elm tree detects the saliva of leaf-eating caterpillars and launches defensive measures by deploying chemicals in the air to attract parasitic wasps. The wasps smell the chemicals and respond by laying their eggs within the bodies of the caterpillars. As the wasp larvae hatch, they devour the body of their host insect from the inside, saving the tree from further harm.

When aphids or other insects gorge on an oak's leaves, the tree sends electrical signals through its fungal partners to warn neighboring trees. When other oaks receive the distress call, they all pump a bitter-tasting chemical called tannin into their leaves to ward off the insects.

If an umbrella thorn acacia in Africa senses an animal munching its branches, it also pumps tannins into its leaves, enough to give even a giraffe an upset stomach. Within minutes, the giraffe moves on. But the giraffe must walk a bit to find another tasty meal. While arming its own defense, the acacia tree released ethylene gas to warn the neighbors. Trees within three hundred feet received the alarm and have already released their tannins.

We Are Like Wizards

Below our canopy of branches
summer heat gives way to shade.
Come windblown seed and creeping vine,
come mushroom, moss, and orchid.
Plant yourself in the rich, moist soil
our decaying leaves provide.
Come tiny mouse and long-legged monkey,
come snake, parrot, and jaguar.
You are welcome to share
the climate we create.
We clean the air and seed the clouds,
we drench the thirsty land with rain.
We are like wizards.

Creating a Climate

The branches of a two-hundred-foot-tall kapok tree reach toward its neighboring trees to form a dense canopy, shading the ground and cooling the air of the Brazilian rain forest.

Groups of trees become an ecosystem, establishing their own local climate. In summer, an average square mile of trees can absorb up to sixteen thousand cubic yards of water per day through their roots and release it as vapor through their leaves. This is enough water to fill two hundred backyard swimming pools. This water vapor accumulates into clouds and eventually falls as rain over the forest and neighboring areas, cooling the air and bringing water to other plants. Decaying leaves and needles build up soil, which, in turn, retains more moisture.

But trees do more to help our climate than just cooling the air and preserving moisture. Through photosynthesis they add oxygen to the air and clean out pollutants. Trees absorb carbon dioxide, ground-level ozone, carbon monoxide, sulfur dioxide, and other greenhouse gases. The forests of the world act as our planet's air filter and lessen the impacts of global warming.

Song of Hunger

The sounds you hear
are the melodies of birds
and wind and rattling limbs.
But there is another song of the forest.
It is a song only my fellow trees will hear.

Helping a Friend

Within the rain forest of British Columbia, Canada, a sickened Douglas fir calls for help from neighboring paper birches and western hemlocks through the Wood Wide Web.

When an injury or disease prevents a tree from being able to produce enough food, it declares its need to the forest. Nearby trees respond by sending sugars along their roots to the distressed tree. This may give it time to regrow until it's able to make enough food on its own.

For a long time, scientists thought trees competed in a forest, but we now know they help one another, even species different from themselves. Canadian scientist Suzanne Simard discovered this when she noticed Douglas fir saplings weakening and dying in a planted forest. Foresters had recently weeded out the paper birches growing among the firs because they thought the birches were competing for resources. But through experiments, Simard discovered that the birch trees had actually been producing enough food for themselves and sharing it with the young firs. Removing them had jeopardized the firs' survival.

electrical signals requesting food

sugars sent to help

15

We Feed a Forest

Our fallen beech nuts, rich in fat,
feed the deer,
the fox, the bear,
and wild boar.
But we must have beech nuts
enough to raise our daughters,
so patiently we plan.
This will be the year
there will be plenty
for the deer,
the fox, the bear,
and wild boar,
with some leftover
to lie undisturbed
before growing into trees.

Super Bloom Years

In a New Hampshire hardwood forest, in eastern USA, beech trees feed many different animals and birds.

To reproduce, many trees (including oaks, beech, and hickory) grow flowers that mature into nuts. But nuts are often eaten by animals. So the trees respond by producing fewer flowers most years to keep the animal population within a healthy limit, and coordinate to produce more flowers—a super bloom—once every three to five years to yield a huge number of nuts. During super bloom years, more nuts will survive to grow into trees.

Our understanding of tree communities is so new that scientists must develop new terms to describe the tree interrelationships. We now recognize that older trees act as "mothers" to the young "daughter" trees that grow from their seeds or nuts.

Like the Bear

All summer we store up food
within our bodies, like the bear.
She feeds on fish, and berries, and fallen nuts.
We feed on rain and sun.
As the autumn light slants low,
the water will slow within our veins
just as the bear's heartbeat slows
when the cold comes creeping in.
Once our leaves have turned to gold
and rattle in the wind,
we will be asleep, like the bear,
safe within her den.

Trees Prepare to Sleep

A black bear finds the perfect location to dig her den under the roots of an old chestnut oak growing on a Virginia mountain.

The tree is also preparing for winter, conserving its energy for when more food and water will be available. Like all trees in cold-winter climates, the oak has been hardening off during the fall, undergoing changes in its cells to protect it from freezing and drying out in the cold. Without this process, water within the trunk and limbs would freeze and expand, bursting wood tissue like frozen water bursts pipes in a house.

cork layer

Deciduous trees like the chestnut oak are designed to shed all their leaves each year. As the tree hardens, it grows a cork-like layer of cells that seal off and weaken the connection between the leaves and branches. Lacking fresh nutrients and water, the leaves cannot produce chlorophyll, the green pigment that absorbs light to make food during photosynthesis. Once the chlorophyll is gone, the remaining pigments in the leaves paint the forest in browns, golds, and reds.

Most coniferous trees also undergo hardening, but their needle-shaped or scale-like leaves remain green in winter. The needles contain antifreeze and sport a waxy coat that protects them from drying out and dying in the cold.

Shhh . . .

We will tell you the rest
of our story in a warmer season,
when the soft white petals of flowers
push through the black soil at our feet
and the wings of moths
tickle our leaves. But for now,
be still and quiet. Find yourself
something else to do.
We are sleeping.

Winter Dormancy

Brittle, sealed-off leaves of deciduous trees often fall in the first strong winds. Leafless trees, like this forest of silver birch in the Xinjiang region of northwest China, can appear to be dead, but they are only dormant, reserving their energy until thawing temperatures permit them to make food again.

By shedding old leaves, trees limit where snow and ice collect on their branches. The combined leaves of a mature maple can consist of twenty thousand square feet of surface area—that's enough to cover a third of a football field! Without all those leaves, a tree is much less susceptible to toppling over or having its limbs break under the weight of heavy snow and ice.

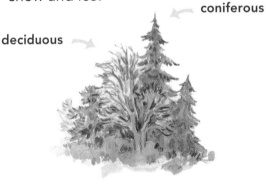

deciduous coniferous

Coniferous trees also experience dormancy with very limited food production. Their pyramid shape and flexible branches help them shed heavy snow.

In both deciduous and coniferous trees, tiny buds that developed last summer are protected from freezing by a thick, scaly coat. They will sprout new growth next spring.

21

Awakening

Sun
sun,
glowing sun,
in spring, our buds sense
lengthening days
and restore our coats of green.
Sun
sun,
warming sun,
our daughter seeds awaken.
They pierce the surface of the soil
and unfurl their trembling leaves.

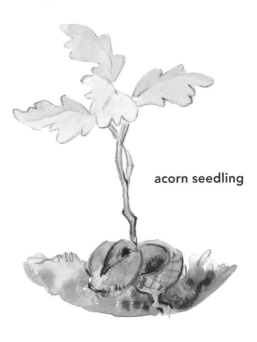

acorn seedling

Telling Time

Some trees, like this sessile oak growing in the Vosges Mountains of France, prepare for seasonal changes by telling time. They don't use a clock; they use light.

In the fall, a blue-green pigment called phytochrome tells trees that it's time to start hardening off for winter because the hours of darkness are lengthening. In spring, the same pigment tells trees that the hours of daylight are lengthening and that it is safe to awaken, flower, and unfurl their leaves. Telling time ensures that these trees won't be tricked into blooming or opening their leaves too soon during an early winter thaw. Other trees that tell time include aspen, cherry, and beech.

Warming winters due to climate change put trees that don't tell time at risk. Birch and hazelnut, trees which react to warming days rather than daylight hours, sometimes lose their blooms due to frost following unseasonal winter warm spells.

We Are the Waiting

We are the saplings, the patient ones.
Decades stretch out ahead as we climb up
from the darkness of the forest floor,
our bright leaves reaching for the light.
Someday we will make our own food
by drinking in the sun. Until then,
warm sugars from our mother's leaves
flow down to us. We are one.

Feeding Younger Trees

Young saplings, like these of the tualang tree in Malaysia, face a tough challenge. They cannot make enough food for themselves, because only about three percent of available sunlight reaches them on the dense forest floor. They also have fewer leaves to gather carbon dioxide. Instead, like other saplings, they rely on the mother trees to share their nutrients through the fungal network. Canadian scientist Suzanne Simard has discovered that mother trees recognize "kin" that are directly related to them and will send more food to kin seedlings than to unrelated seedlings.

Trees produce food, in the form of sugar, for themselves and their mycorrhizal fungi through photosynthesis. In this process, chlorophyll in their leaves traps energy from the sun. The tree uses the energy to convert carbon dioxide and water into the sugar glucose, releasing oxygen into the air in the process.

photosynthesis

sunlight and carbon dioxide absorbed through leaves

oxygen exhaled through leaves

sugar synthesized

water absorbed through roots

minerals absorbed through fungi

We Are the Lofty

Slender, bending,
strong, and tall,
with limbs that touch.
Each of us breathes in
the sharp, fresh taste of air.
We have found our place,
to dance among the stars.

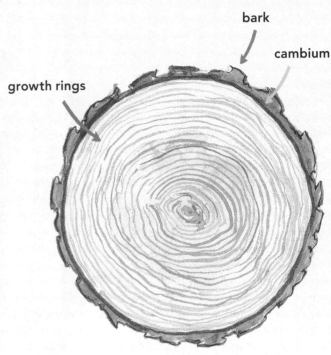

bark

cambium

growth rings

Tree Growth

Like humans, trees grow taller as they mature until they reach their full height. These pignut hickory living in Michigan, USA, have grown ninety feet tall. But once they sense neighboring trees, they will stop lengthening their branches. This ensures that every tree in the community can gather sunlight without competition.

Even after they stop growing taller, the branches and trunk of a tree continue to get wider their entire lives. With each new year, trees add a light and dark growth ring as the cambium, the thin layer between the bark and wood, grows new woody cells on the inside and new bark cells on the outside. Light rings form in the spring and are generally wider when ample moisture allows faster growth. Dark rings are thinner and form as growth slows down in late summer and fall. You can discover the age of a tree by counting the number of dark or light rings. If a tree has one hundred dark rings, it is one hundred years old.

More Than Just Ourselves

Rustle of leaf, stretch of legs,
a spider unhooks from an uppermost limb.
Leaps, then glides on windless air
building a gossamer web.
Wiggle, chirp, eyes still closed,
robin chicks rest within twig woven nest.
Whir of wing, parents return
bearing a beak full of food.
Bang, bang, chisel, build a new home,
a woodpecker pair climbs inside.
Relax, heads tucked into feathers.
Soon there will be eggs to protect.
Whimper, whine, faces peer out.
Mother raccoon grows impatient.
One timid kit crawls from a hollow
balanced on leaf-covered limbs.
Sniff, sniff, streak of red,
a mother fox crawls under our roots.
Paws folded, yawn, lick.
Her kits asleep in their den.

Trees Create Homes

The body of this sugar maple growing in Vermont, USA, provides safety and shelter to countless wildlife and thousands of insects. Baby birds such as crows, blue jays, and warblers are born in nests built from leaves and twigs. Porcupines, bats, and fishers sleep on leaf-shaded branches. Others live in cavities within the tree. Most animals don't harm the trees they live in.

Cavity homes are created in many trees when a branch breaks and a gap in the protective layer of bark opens. Over time wood-decay fungi (different from the fungi that live in partnership with tree roots) invade the spot. Wood-decay fungi digest moist wood, causing it to rot, allowing insects to burrow and feed. With passing years, the size of the cavity grows, creating homes for larger animals like owls, raccoons, and even bears. Trees can live for centuries with these cavities, but eventually they weaken from the invading fungi. The soft wood of weakened trees allows woodpeckers to chisel out new holes each year. After they move out, squirrels, wood ducks, chickadees, and other animals move in.

The number of insects living and feeding on one tree is almost too vast to count, but scientists have studied individual trees intensely to discover just how many different kinds of insects certain trees can support. The record so far is over four thousand different species living in one kapok tree in Costa Rica.

We Are the Ancient

For hundreds
of years we have taken
our turn to block the wind, and help
our fellow trees. We have survived drought,
disease, and blizzard storms.
Now it's time
to rest.

Helping the Ancient Ones

Some species of trees live for a really long time. This European yew, named Ankerwycke, on the River Thames west of London, may be 2,500 years old. Local lore claims Henry VIII met his second wife, Anne Boleyn, under its great boughs. But trees need help if they are to grow to be this ancient.

After centuries of adding width, tree branches take on a gnarled look, like arthritic hands. And just as humans experience thinning hair as they age, a tree's branches become sparse as it grows older because the tree can't support ever widening limbs that have grown too heavy. Older branches are broken by wind and ice storms, until eventually only a few limbs and trunk remain. Fewer branches mean fewer leaves, and the tree's energy level drops. Wood-decay fungi invade, breaking down the wood and hollowing out the trunks. These ancient ones can no longer produce enough food on their own and rely on their daughter trees and neighbors for aid.

wood-decay fungus

We Are the Ghosts

My limbs and needles are gone,
and the warm body of a newborn deer
comes to rest within the ghost of my great trunk
that once touched the sky.
But underneath the soft litter
of fallen needles and dark soil, I still live,
surrounded by my kingdom
with their willingness to give.

Life Beyond Death

A forest may continue to care for its elder trees, even after the body of an ancient tree dies aboveground. The roots are still alive and remain a part of the community. When this five-hundred-year-old ponderosa pine fell in eastern Oregon, USA, its trunk and branches began decomposing, sending its stored nutrients back into the soil, while its roots continued to bring in water. The hollowed-out trunk became shelter to many animals. Nearby younger trees, exposed to more sunlight, grew quickly to fill in the forest canopy. Now, many years later, the ancient remains of the tree are still a part of the community.

root circle

The remains of long-gone beech trees look like moss-covered stones laid out in a large circle. But these aren't stones; they are roots pushing to the surface, outlining the width of a former tree trunk, rotted centuries before but still alive belowground as nearby trees share the food they make with their fallen member.

33

We Are a Village

Our forest is woven
from a diversity of trees.
The oak,
the juniper,
the alder,
the aspen.
The spruce,
the maple,
the fir,
the pine,
each of us serves a purpose
in the rich fabric of life.

The Importance of Diversity

Healthy forests, like this one in Colorado, USA, need tree diversity to fight off disease and insect predation. If one species of tree is targeted by insects, others will survive because different trees employ different defensive strategies. Unfortunately, many naturally diverse forests of the world have been made less diverse by humans. Logged old-growth forests are replaced by newly planted saplings. These planted forests resemble farms with a single crop rather than a healthy, rich, diverse ecosystem.

Uniform forests can fall victim to massive, widespread death, especially in changing climate, such as increasingly frequent drought conditions. North American forests composed almost entirely of lodgepole or ponderosa pine are being wiped out by the mountain pine beetle, and forests of Engelmann spruce have been devastated by spruce beetles. Ninety-two thousand square miles of forest (larger than the state of Utah) in the western United States have been ravaged since 2000. The vast amount of dead trees leaves animals without food and the area susceptible to intense wildfires and soil erosion, causing even more devastation.

Tree diversity leads to healthier forests and helps multiple species of wildlife thrive by providing a wide range of food and homes. Keeping our forests alive also combats rising greenhouse gases. Trees are our planet's best defense against climate change.

AUTHOR'S NOTE

Years ago, on a hiking trip, I sat under a thousand-year-old oak that overlooked a medieval English castle. I listened to the bleating of lambs that surrounded me and wondered about the history this ancient tree must have witnessed: religious pilgrims walking by on their way to a neighboring abbey, the surviving wife of Henry VIII ending her days here, Charles I finding refuge during England's civil war while battles were fought nearby. And then the castle lay neglected for two centuries. The cast of characters that came to life for me under its limbs felt as genuine as anything that existed in reality. I was tired from my hike and thinking about what I wanted to do in life. I sat quietly with the tree, pressed my back to it, and felt a growing joy take hold. Was it the tree's wisdom that seeped into my body, or the sanctuary it provided, allowing me to feel my own? Eventually I could almost sense the tree whispering what I needed to hear—to stop just imagining other people's tales and begin to write my own. The trunk, upright and solid, lent me support. I went home, quit my job, and wrote my first book.

I return to that tree as often as I can to sit under its limbs and give thanks. But now I've learned that this great oak, which I have loved like a friend, has its own stories to tell, far more surprising and breathtaking than I could have ever imagined.

MORE ABOUT FUNGI

Genetically, fungi are more closely related to animals than plants, though they are neither and belong to their own kingdom classification for living organisms. With about 144,000 known species, they are one of the most widely distributed organisms on the planet. Types of fungi include yeasts, rusts, smuts, mildews, molds, and mushrooms. Many live on their own in soil or water, while others form either a symbiotic or parasitic relationship with plants or animals.

Symbiotic fungi live in close relationship with trees by colonizing in their roots (page 9, "Secrets of the Wood Wide Web"). This relationship between host plant and fungus is called a mycorrhiza. There are mycorrhizal fungi living in the roots of about 95 percent of all green plants, not just trees.

Parasitic fungi living on trees are known as wood-decay fungi. Some of these fungal species (as in the fungi depicted on page 31, "Helping the Ancient Ones") consume and break down dead trees, while others digest living wood tissue, causing trees to rot. Wood-decay fungi can hollow out tree trunks and eventually kill them. Some of these wood-decay fungi live both above and below the ground, growing to become the largest organisms on the planet. The largest of all is a honey fungus growing in the Blue Mountains of Oregon. Aboveground it takes the shape of mushrooms, while belowground, hollow, black, tentacle-shaped fingers spread out to feed on living wood. At its widest point, this single fungus reaches two and a half miles and has been feeding off trees for an estimated 2,400 years. In total it covers nearly four square miles. If it could all be put on a scale, scientists estimate it would weigh more than 7,500 tons!

HOW LONG DO TREES LIVE?

Different species of trees have different life spans. Some trees are relatively short lived, like the paper birch, which lives far less than two hundred years. Others, like giant sequoias and Great Basin bristlecone pines, can live a few thousand years.

Some tree species literally reproduce themselves, forming a clonal colony that can grow into the oldest life-forms on earth. These trees send up shoots from their roots that grow into genetically identical clones of the original tree. Aboveground the trees appear to be distinct individuals, but underground they share the same root system, and since they all contain the same genetics, they are all considered one organism. One tree may live for only a short while, but the colony itself can thrive for a mind-blowing length of time. One such stand of Huon pine trees on the west coast of Tasmania is likely to be over 10,500 years old. A colony of quaking aspen in Utah, nicknamed Pando, contains forty-seven thousand identical trees and is estimated to be around twelve thousand years old!

THE TREES IN THIS BOOK

For hundreds of millions of years trees have been living in cooperation with one another, but forest ecologists have been decoding their private and mysterious lives for only the past twenty years. Much of the research available to me in writing this book was specifically focused on studies of North American and European forests. It would be impossible to mention the more than sixty thousand tree species around the world, but scientists are learning that all trees live in deep connection with one another. I chose as wide a selection as I could to show their geographic diversity and individual beauty.

HALF TITLE PAGE

Southern live oak trees grow in coastal regions of the southeastern United States and are rarely found more than three hundred feet above sea level. They live for hundreds of years, growing one to two feet a year to reach up to eighty feet in height. They are wonderful shade trees, spreading their limbs sixty to a hundred feet wide. Because of their extra-deep and widespread root system, they can survive strong, sustained winds, such as those seen in hurricanes.

On the half title page, I depicted a grove on Saint Simons Island, Georgia. Live oaks from the island were harvested for their exceptionally hard, heavy wood in the 1790s to build some of the first ships for the United States Navy. One of the most famous, the USS *Constitution*, was nicknamed "Old Ironsides" after surviving cannon fire due to its incredibly strong hull.

FULL TITLE PAGE

Some individuals of Great Basin bristlecone pine are the oldest trees on earth. According to the measurements taken by scientist Tom Harlan, one of these trees is 4,851 years old. The tree is named Methuselah, but its exact location is guarded as a secret to prevent vandalism. Other trees in this area are also suspected to be approaching five thousand years old. These ancient pines are adapted to live under extreme conditions and are found only at high elevations in Utah, Nevada, and eastern California. They live where most other plants can't grow, thriving in rocky soil with virtually no rainfall. Because of freezing temperatures, dry soils, high winds, and short growing seasons, the trees grow very slowly.

A SECRET KINGDOM

Ancient woodlands containing common, or European, beech were once widespread throughout Europe. Today unspoiled beech forests with mature, three-hundred-year-old trees are found only in small pockets like the Ruhe Forest in Hümmel, Germany. Beeches are still a common tree today, but planted in isolation, away from native forests, they live only half their life expectancy.

The leaves of beech trees, like some sycamores and oaks, do not drop in fall after turning copper and gold. Instead they remain on the tree until the spring, just before new leaves open.

HOW TO SPEAK IN TREE

Mixed forests of Douglas fir, balsam fir, western hemlock, and western red cedar growing along the coastal mountains of British Columbia, Canada, form a temperate rain forest. As their name implies, temperate rain forests are much cooler than their tropical counterparts. They are home to an incredible amount of biological productivity, storing up to 880 tons of leaves, wood, and other organic matter per acre.

The province of British Columbia is making great efforts to stop deforestation because healthy forests in these regions are extremely important for biodiversity and preserving clean air. In 2010, the government passed the Zero Net Deforestation Act. The plan states that for any area that is deforested and permanently cleared, an equal-sized area of unforested land will be planted with trees. This would create a "net zero" effect on deforestation.

NEIGHBOR, CAN YOU HEAR ME?

The American elms living in Central Park in New York City are historically significant—they are one of the largest and last remaining stands of American elm trees in North America. Once a dominant species in much of midwestern and eastern North America, elms were a popular tree planted in town parks and along roads for the abundance of shade their wide canopies provided. While elms have evolved the remarkable ability to defend themselves against native caterpillars, as described on page 11, they have no defense against diseases introduced from regions where elms did not evolve.

In the last century, elms all over America and Europe have been devastated by fungi that are spread by elm bark beetles. Due to extensive research by the Dutch, it became known as Dutch elm disease. Scientists believe the fungi originated in Asia, and it was traced to logs imported from Europe to make furniture. It has been estimated that hundreds of millions of elms have been killed by Dutch elm disease. Scientists continue to look for ways to stop the disease, but all remaining American elms are still vulnerable.

The umbrella thorn acacia tree depicted in the sidebar on page 11 grows throughout Serengeti National Park in Tanzania, Africa, where the Masai giraffe lives. The giraffes prefer to eat acacia's sweet leaves, despite the long thorns on the branches. Giraffes have evolved very long faces to avoid getting poked in the eye while eating.

WE ARE LIKE WIZARDS

Kapok trees are the giants of rain forests from southern Mexico to the southern Amazon. They grow as much as thirteen feet a year to reach heights up to two hundred feet and preside over a diverse forest community. In the two and half acres of rain forest around a kapok tree, two hundred

different kinds of smaller trees can grow. And all that diversity supports forty-two thousand different species of insects.

Kapok trees are drought deciduous and shed their leaves during the dry season. Every few years after the leaves drop, they produce flowers that bats pollinate at night. These grow into woody seedpods that split open while still on the tree, exposing the white, fluffy fiber inside to the breeze and dispersing the seeds. The fiber is buoyant and water-resistant, and people use it to stuff pillows, mattresses, and life preservers. People also use the seeds, leaves, bark, and sap as medicine to treat dysentery, fever, asthma, and kidney disease.

SONG OF HUNGER

If given a chance to live its full lifetime of a thousand years, a Douglas fir could possibly reach heights of four hundred feet or more, making it the tallest tree species in the world. But no four hundred footers are known to exist today because people have logged Douglas fir extensively. Replacement trees have been planted in vast plantations to provide lumber for construction. Because of its commercial value, Douglas fir has been introduced in plantations in Europe, Argentina, Chile, and New Zealand, sometimes becoming an invasive threat to native trees.

Paper birches are cut for pulpwood and firewood. They live 80 to 140 years in a forest, but planted in yards where they are cut off from the fungal network, they live only about thirty years.

Forest ecologists, like Suzanne Simard, are now learning that the common practice of clear-cutting forests and planting all new saplings is an unwise method of regenerating forests. Foresters are now beginning to recognize that it would be better to leave healthy clumps of trees within cut areas so that their networks can link with new saplings.

WE FEED A FOREST

The American beech is a deciduous tree growing to 115 feet tall, with smooth, silver-gray bark. It is native to eastern North America, west to Wisconsin and south to eastern Texas. Beech trees are one of the last trees to establish in a forest. Part of the reason is that they are very shade tolerant, and saplings can grow in a mature forest more easily than other species. Once established, they form a stable ecosystem and can dominate a forest. Before the colonists arrived, four-hundred-year-old trees grew in mature beech forests, but today the oldest known American beech is probably no more than 270 years old.

LIKE THE BEAR

Chestnut oaks are sometimes called rock oaks because they grow on rocky ridges, mostly in the eastern United States, with an outlying population in southern Michigan. In the Appalachian Mountains, hollow chestnut oaks are a favorite place for black bears to make their dens. Sometimes they use cavities at the base of the tree, but often they choose cavities high up, where they're less likely to be disturbed.

It takes at least fifty years for chestnut oaks to grow big enough for a bear to fit inside a trunk. They are not fast growers, but chestnut oaks will eventually reach about seventy feet with a similar spread and can live for three hundred years or more. The trees have silvery gray bark with a high tannin content, and up until the twentieth century, it was used to tan leather. People also use the wood for fence posts and railroad ties because the tannin makes it fairly rot resistant.

SHHH . . .

On page 21, a Eurasian wolf walks silently through a dormant forest of silver birch in the Xinjiang region of China. Silver birch are medium-sized deciduous trees that typically grow to eighty feet tall with slender trunks usually no more than sixteen inches in diameter. They owe their name to the white peeling bark on their trunks. In spring, flowers in the form of catkins mature into winged seeds that are scattered by the wind. These trees prefer cold climates and are native throughout much of Europe and Asia. They are often the dominant forest tree in areas where temperatures remain freezing most of the year.

Silver birch are a pioneer species, which means they are one of the first trees to appear in open land and start a new forest. Their sparse crown lets light reach the ground, allowing many plants and shrubs to grow beneath their limbs.

AWAKENING

There are over five hundred species of oak trees worldwide. The sessile oak shown on pages 22–23 is native to hilly regions throughout most of Europe to the Caucasus Mountains in Asia.

Sessile oak can grow up to 130 feet tall, and like other oaks, it is known for its exceptionally hard, heavy wood. It was prized for ship building until the mid-nineteenth century, and remains a popular wood for architectural beams. For centuries people used the leaves, bark, and acorns to treat many medical ailments, including digestive problems and kidney stones. Today sessile oaks are used to make floors, furniture, and wine barrels. Winemakers have found that the wood from sessile oaks has fewer bitter tannins and more sweet chemical compounds than other oaks used to make wine barrels.

WE ARE THE WAITING

The tualang is the tallest tree in the tropical rain forests of Indonesia, Malaysia, the Philippines, and Thailand. One is measured today at 289 feet. Like most rain forest giants, they have huge buttress roots to support their weight. The roots spread out wide rather than dig deep because most of the nutrients in rain forest soil are very near the surface.

Tualang trees are home to Asian rock bees, the world's largest honeybee. For this reason, the trees are protected by law from being cut down in many areas. Large disk-shaped honeycombs hang from horizontal branches high in the trees. One tualang can hold more than a hundred honeycombs, each reaching six feet across and containing as many as thirty thousand bees. Malaysian locals nail wooden ladders to climb the trees and harvest the honey without harming the tree. The honey is known to have antioxidant properties and is used traditionally for the treatment of various diseases.

WE ARE THE LOFTY

Pignut hickory trees like the ones on pages 26–27 grow in humid climates of the Midwest and eastern United States and Canada. They can grow to a hundred feet tall, but fifty to sixty feet is more typical. They're called pignut because wild hogs feed on the nuts.

The tree's wood, however, is more highly valued. In pioneer days, the very strong, dense wood was used to make wagon wheels because it could withstand tremendous vibration. Hickory was once a popular choice for baseball bats, used by such legends as Shoeless Joe Jackson and Babe Ruth, but by the 1930s players favored lighter bats made of ash and maple. Today pignut hickory is used to make tool handles, ladder rungs, and flooring.

MORE THAN JUST OURSELVES

Sugar maples, on pages 28–29, are very popular in eastern North American forests for their bright red, yellow, and orange fall foliage and for being the primary source of maple syrup. The trees grow slowly and can live a few hundred years in a forest, reaching over a hundred feet tall with a dense, rounded crown that provides plenty of shade. The twigs, leaves, and buds are browsed by white-tailed deer, moose, snowshoe hare, and squirrels. Squirrels and birds also eat the seeds. Like beech and oak, sugar maples have a super bloom every two to five years.

The wood is hard, heavy, and durable. It is well suited for furniture, flooring, and veneer. You'll find it in basketball courts, bowling pins and alleys, baseball bats, and musical instruments.

WE ARE THE ANCIENT

It's hard to determine the age of yews through the conventional means of counting growth rings. The trunks of yews tend to hollow out after about four hundred years. So scientists estimate the age by studying the growth rate of nearby trees and looking at the archaeological evidence under and around the ancient roots. This evidence shows that European yews are among the oldest plants on earth, some reaching 3,500 years in age. Many of the oldest yews are found near churchyards and historical sites, where they have been protected. The Ankerwycke yew, pictured on pages 30–31, for example, is close to the ruins of Saint Mary's Priory, a nunnery built in the twelfth century across the river from Runnymede meadow. Some say that by this already ancient yew in 1215, King John sealed the Magna Carta, the influential document that made the king subject to the law and guaranteed justice and a fair trial to free men.

Different kinds of yews live around the world. European yews range throughout Europe and North Africa. Others live in Asia. The bark of one North American species, the Pacific yew, was used to develop the drug Taxol, which treats several different cancers.

WE ARE THE GHOSTS

The ponderosa pine depicted on pages 32–33 lived five hundred years before the aboveground tree died and fell. It had a long, deep root system that allowed the tree to access moisture far belowground, enabling it to grow in the arid conditions of eastern Oregon. Ponderosas are native to western North America. Deep roots keep these trees in place even in the strongest winds, so they often remain standing long after death. They are a perfect snag tree for wildlife and insect homes. In spring, the outer bark of ponderosa pines can be peeled away when the sap runs thick with sugar, and the thin inner bark layer can be eaten. Their massive trunks can be hollowed out to make dugout canoes. The pitch, the sticky substance pines produce to cover their wounds, can be used for waterproofing shoes and containers, and as an ointment for sores and inflamed eyes.

The circle of roots depicted in the sidebar on page 33 are those of an ancient beech within the Ruhe Forest in Hümmel, Germany. The entire body of the aboveground tree has decayed and turned into soil, a clear indication that the tree must have fallen more than fifty years earlier.

WE ARE A VILLAGE

The more than twenty-four million acres of forest in Colorado provide vital shelter for wildlife, improve water quality, and filter pollutants from the air. The diverse landscape includes a variety of trees: Gambel oak, Rocky Mountain juniper, thinleaf alder, quaking aspen, blue spruce, Rocky Mountain maple, box elder, chokecherry, lodgepole pine, Douglas fir. But even though Colorado forests are diverse, historical studies show that modern land management has considerably altered their makeup. Forests 150 years ago were more open with a mix of grassland and clumps of trees of different ages.

Over time, policies to put out any fire (known as fire suppression) had resulted in a crowded forest, with fewer old-growth trees. This increases the potential for severe wildfires, insect damage, and disease. Many western woodlands have already suffered dramatically from these ill effects. Scientists, nonprofit environmental organizations, and government agencies are now recognizing the need to address this issue. Together these organizations have identified areas to restore to more natural conditions in hopes of enhancing forest health and resilience.

FOREST FIRE SUPPRESSION

Naturally occurring fires, started by lightning strikes, are common in forests. In a healthy, moist ecosystem, fires burn fuels such as grasses, dead wood, leaves, pine needles, and twigs. They die out before harming large trees. Frequent, small fires keep fuel from accumulating. But when people suppress forest fires, fuels accumulate. Fires burn hotter, flaming up into forest canopies. They jump from tree to tree over wide areas and cause mass devastation.

Despite our growing understanding that small natural blazes are part of a healthy ecosystem, the continued spread of houses into forested areas means there is growing pressure to suppress the fires. More people in these areas also means more fires start from cigarette butts, campfires, arson, even pieces of littered glass concentrating the sun's rays. The rising temperatures and drought that come with climate change only worsen the situation. The result is a marked increase in the number of massive, devastating fires on our planet.

THE FUTURE OF OUR FORESTS

We have already lost 46 percent of the world's trees since the start of human civilization, and at the current pace of deforestation, we are losing more than two trees per person per year. At this rate, we will lose 50 percent of the earth's remaining trees in the next hundred years. The destruction of the globe's forests is resulting in significant numbers of plants and animals becoming threatened or extinct. We are also losing the potential for new medical treatments. More than 40 percent of prescription drugs prescribed by Western doctors alone are now derived from plants and trees. By cutting down our forests, we are limiting the number of lifesaving treatments that could be discovered.

If we are to stem global warming, deforestation must stop, and replanting with tree diversity in mind must begin. Replanting lands devastated by logging and natural disasters will increase tree cover to absorb carbon dioxide from the atmosphere, lower air temperature, protect biodiversity, and preserve clean water sources. Reforestation is particularly important across the tropics and subtropics where trees grow quickly.

Measures have already begun to accomplish this. The Bonn Challenge is a global effort to restore deforested and degraded land. Currently fifty-nine countries, including many across the tropics and subtropics, such as Brazil, India, and China, have committed land to reforestation by the year 2030. Other conservation organizations such as the World Wildlife Fund, Wildlife Conservation Society, and BirdLife International have called for an initiative to restore one trillion trees by 2050.

HOW YOU CAN HELP OUR FORESTS

★ Reduce. Reuse. Recycle. If we recycle the products that come from trees, such as paper, we can lower the demand to cut more trees.

★ Buy from companies that are environment friendly. Read their environmental policies to determine whether they follow sustainable use practices.

★ Make informed food choices. Every year forested land is cleared for grazing livestock. Reducing your consumption of meat and dairy products can help save forests.

★ Buy products made from recycled materials.

★ Read newspapers or magazines online rather than buying the paper form.

★ Buy furniture and wood that is certified by the Forest Stewardship Council, which confirms that the wood in a product was legally cut down.

★ Educate your friends and family about how trees help our planet, and how our actions affect forests around the world.

★ Plant native trees in your yard and don't cut down standing snags. Both provide homes for wildlife. Trees native to your region will promote healthy insect diversity.

A NOTE FROM THE PUBLISHER

At Macmillan, we take great pride in the work we do. We believe that in partnering with authors to publish their great books, we are changing millions of lives for the better through education, stirring the imagination, and providing satisfying reading experiences. We strongly believe that creating a sustainable future is necessary not only in our business but also for our world. Sustainability has become part of our everyday discussion and a key factor in our business decisions. The biggest area of environmental impact for a book publisher remains paper consumption. Paper, combined with the transportation, printing, and distribution of books, accounts for over 80 percent of Macmillan's carbon footprint. We have worked hard to reduce our emissions from our directly purchased paper and continue to look for other ways to reduce our emissions. We also have a strong paper sourcing policy and invite you to review it on macmillansustainability.com.

GLOSSARY

canopy—The top layer of a forest, formed by the spreading branches of leafy trees.

chlorophyll—The green pigment that absorbs light to provide energy for photosynthesis.

coniferous—Trees or shrubs that produce seed cones. They are mostly evergreen and have needles or scales for leaves.

crown—The branches and leaves at the top of a tree's trunk.

decay—To rot or decompose through the action of bacteria and fungi.

deciduous—Trees or shrubs that shed their leaves seasonally.

dormancy—The period when plants stop growing and making food to conserve energy during unfavorable conditions.

ecosystem—A community of interacting organisms and their environment.

forest—An unfarmed, wooded area of at least two and a half acres with a tree canopy covering more than 10 percent.

hardwood forest—Forests composed of deciduous trees.

larvae—The wingless and often wormlike feeding form of an immature insect after it emerges from an egg.

mycorrhiza—The association of a fungus with the roots of a plant.

parasitic—Living in, with, or on an organism to obtain benefits from it, usually causing it harm.

phytochrome—Plant pigment that measures light and regulates plant growth.

pigment—Chemical compounds that absorb different wavelengths of light, producing different colors.

sapling—A young tree, especially one with a slender trunk.

snag—A standing dead or dying tree.

symbiotic—Involving interaction between two different organisms living in close physical association, usually resulting in a mutually beneficial relationship.

tannin—Astringent chemicals plants produce to deter animals from eating them.

Wood Wide Web—The underground network of mycorrhizal fungi that connect tree roots.

SOURCES

Casselman, Anne. "Strange but True: The Largest Organism on Earth Is a Fungus." *Scientific American,* Oct. 4, 2007. scientificamerican.com/article/strange-but-true-largest-organism-is-fungus/.

Crowther, T. W., H. B. Glick, K. R. Covey, C. Bettigole, D. S. Maynard, S. M. Thomas, J. R. Smith et al. "Mapping Tree Density at a Global Scale." *Nature* 525 (Sept. 2, 2015): 201–205. doi.org/10.1038/nature14967.

Fleming, Nic. "Plants Talk to Each Other Using an Internet of Fungus." BBC Earth, Nov. 11, 2014. bbc.com/earth/story/20141111-plants-have-a-hidden-internet.

Franklin, Jerry F., and James K. Agee. "Forging a Science-Based National Forest Fire Policy." *Issues in Science and Technology,* July 8, 2019. issues.org/franklin/.

Grant, Michael C. "The Trembling Giant." *Discover Magazine,* Oct. 1, 1993. discovermagazine.com/planet-earth/the-trembling-giant.

Haskell, David George. *The Songs of Trees: Stories from Nature's Great Connectors.* New York: Penguin, 2017.

Pakenham, Thomas. *Remarkable Trees of the World.* New York: Norton, 2003.

Simard, Suzanne W. "Mother Tree." Film by Dan McKinney. Dec. 14, 2011. YouTube. 4:40 mins. youtu.be/-8SORM4dYG8.

Simard, Suzanne W., David A. Perry, Melanie D. Jones, David D. Myrold, Daniel M. Durall, and Randy Molina. "Net Transfer of Carbon Between Ectomycorrhizal Tree Species in the Field." *Nature,* 388 (Aug. 7, 1997): 579–582. doi.org/10.1038/41557.

Toomey, Diane. "Exploring How and Why Trees 'Talk' to Each Other." Interview with Suzanne W. Simard. *Yale Environment 360,* Sept. 1, 2016. e360.yale.edu/features/exploring_how_and_why_trees_talk_to_each_other.

Wohlleben, Peter. *The Hidden Life of Trees: What They Feel, How They Communicate; Discoveries from a Secret World.* Translated by Jane Billinghurst. Vancouver, BC: Greystone Books, 2016.

GOOD WEBSITES FOR MORE INFORMATION ON TREES AND FORESTS

American Forests: americanforests.org
Plant-for-the-Planet: plant-for-the-planet.org
Rainforest Alliance: rainforest-alliance.org
Bonn Challenge: BonnChallenge.org
Trillion Trees campaign: 1t.org and trilliontrees.org
Trees for Cities: treesforcities.org